New Music Matters 11-14

2

Chris Hiscock and Marian Metcalfe

Heinemann

Heinemann Educational Publishers
Halley Court, Jordan Hill, Oxford OX2 8EJ
Part of Harcourt Limited

Heinemann is the registered trademark of Harcourt Education Limited

© Marian Metcalfe and Chris Hiscock 1999

First published 1999

07 06

10

British Library Cataloguing in Publication Data
A catalogue record for this product is available from the British Library

10-digit ISBN: 0 435810 91 X
13-digit ISBN: 978 0 435810 91 7

Typeset and designed by Artistix, Thame, Oxon
Music typesetting by Halstan & Co., Amersham, Bucks
Printed and bound in Spain by Edelvives
Cover design by The Point

Acknowledgements

Grateful thanks are extended to Chris McGeever, Hampden Park School and Debbie Bennet, Hailsham Community College for help with research and Clare Hiscock for general support, help and encouragement.

The publishers would like to thank the following for permission to reproduce copyright material:
Let's Dance words and music by Jim Lee © 1957 Rondell Music/Warner-Tamerlane Publishing Corp., USA Warner/Chappell Music Ltd, London W6 8BS. Reproduced by permission of IMP Ltd on pp. 4–8; *Heart and Soul* music by Hoagy Carmichael, words by Frank Loesser © 1938 renewed 1967 Famous Music Corporation, USA. Used by permission of Music Sales Ltd. All rights reserved. International copyright secured, on p. 11; *Earth Angel (Will You Be Mine)* words and music by Jesse Belvin, Gaynel Hodge and Curtis Williams © 1955 Dootsie Williams Inc/Warner Chappell Music Inc., USA Warner/Chappell Music Ltd, London, W6 8BS. Reproduced by permission of IMP Ltd on pp. 14–15; *Balulalow* from *A Ceremony of Carols*, Op. 28 by Britten /Wedderburn © Copyright 1943 by Boosey & Co Ltd. Reproduced by permission of Boosey and Hawkes Music Publishers Ltd on p. 22; *Carillon* by Francis Poulenc reproduced by permission of Editions Durand S.A., Paris/United Music Publishers Ltd on p. 24 and 27; *Happy Hour* words and music by L. Schott and D. Frye © 1927 Peer International Corporation, USA. Peermusic (UK) Limited, 8–14 Verulam Street, London WC1. Used by permission of Music Sales Ltd. All rights reserved. International copyright secured, on p. 28; *Suffolk Morris* by Doreen Carwithen © Doreen Carwithen on pp. 40–42;

Sakura arr. R. W. Mitchell © R. W. Mitchell on p. 50; *Kites* by Pockriss Lee Julien © 1967 Emily Music Corp. and Hackady's Publishing, USA Campbell Connelly & Co. Ltd., 8/9 Frith Sreet, London W1V 5TZ. Used by permission of Music Sales Ltd. All rights reserved. International copyright secured, on p. 54.

The publishers would like to thank the following for permission to reproduce photographs:
p. 9 Hulton Getty; p. 10 (top) Corbis; p. 10 (middle and bottom) Hulton Getty; p. 11 Neal Preston/Corbis; p. 16 Bonhams/Bridgeman; p. 17 Hulton Getty; p. 18 David Lees/Corbis; p. 19 Roberta Parkin/Redferns; p. 23 Key Light; p. 26 (both) Christopher Cormack/Corbis; p. 29 Redferns/Leon Morris; p. 31 (top) Photodisc; p. 31 (bottom) Lebrecht; p. 34 Bridgeman; p. 35 Barnaby's; p. 38 Hobgoblin; p. 39 (top) Don Sutton; p. 39 (bottom) Ted Spiegel/Corbis; p. 41 Adam Woolfitt/Corbis; p. 44 Mary Evans; p. 45 Yoshikazu Iwamoto; p. 46 (left) Victoria & Albert Museum; p. 46 (top right) Monty Levenson; p. 46 (bottom right) Photodisc; p. 48 (top) Michael S. Yamashita/Corbis; p. 48 (bottom) Robbie Jack/Corbis; p. 49 Michael S. Yamashita/Corbis; p. 50 Barnaby's; p. 52 Barnaby's; p. 55 (all) Lebrecht; p. 58 Victoria & Albert Museum; p. 60 Lebrecht; p. 62 (top) Hulton-Deutsch/Corbis; p. 62 (bottom) Bridgeman; p. 64 (left) BBC; p. 64 (right) David Gamble/Sygma.

The publishers have made every effort to contact copyright holders. However, if any material has been incorrectly acknowledged, the publishers would be pleased to correct this at the earliest opportunity.

Contents

Project 1 Chords I, II, IV, V & VI **4**

Let's dance 4

Composing melodies from chords 8

Music and dance in the 1950s 9

Listening to rock 'n' roll music 10

I, VI, IV(II), V scat! 11

Meet chords II and VI 13

Earth Angel 14

Project 2 Using chords in songs **16**

Accompaniments and backings 16

Considering chord patterns 17

Performing chord patterns 18

Listening to O holy night 20

Assessing accompaniments 22

Project 3 Rondos and recurring structures **23**

Carillon 23

More about musical structure 25

Listening to Carillon 26

Happy hour 28

Ritorno 29

Gaudete 30

Listening to a rondo 31

Project 4 $\frac{6}{8}$ and compound time **33**

Using compound time: performing The dargason 36

Some traditional Celtic instruments 38

Listening to traditional Irish music 39

Performing Suffolk morris 40

Listening to Suffolk morris 42

Looking at how composers work 43

Listening to more music in compound time 44

Project 5 Textures and timbres in the music of Japan **45**

Listening to new sounds 46

More about Japanese music 48

Performing Sakura 50

Improvising using the In scale 51

Listening to Etenraku: timbres into textures 52

Etenraku graphic score 53

Kites 54

Project 6 Studying a baroque concerto **55**

Lute concerto in D major by Antonio Vivaldi 55

Lute concerto in D – first movement 56

Improvisations in ritornello form 58

Listening to the first movement 59

Lute concerto in D – second movement 60

Listening to the second movement 62

Listening to the third movement 63

Making comparisons 64

Chords I, II, IV, V & VI

Let's dance

Jim Lee arr. CH

Let's dance is a popular song from the rock 'n' roll era of the 1950s and early 1960s. This arrangement has parts for voices, chords, bass and drums or percussion.

Voice part

1 Hey ba - by won't you take a chance, _ Say that you'll let me
2 Hey ba - by yeah you thrill me so, ___ Hold me tight, don't you
3 Hey ba - by if you're all a - lone, _ May - be you'll let me

have this dance,___ Let's dance, Let's dance,
let me go, ___
walk you home, _

We'll do the twist, the stomp, the mashed po - ta - to too,___

A - ny old dance that you want to do ___ but let's dance,

Last time to Coda Link bars

Let's dance, Ah _____

DS Coda

Ah _____ Let's dance!

The three-chord trick

The **three-chord trick** is a combination of chords I, IV, and V in any key. *Let's dance* uses the three-chord trick in the key of C (chords C, F and G). Practise playing these chords before adding the backing to the melody.

Introducing seventh chords (C7)

During the link/coda sections, a new chord, **C7**, is introduced:

The chord of C7 has four notes: C, E, G, B♭. When 7 is added to a chord symbol it tells us to add the note **one tone below the upper key note**. This note is added to give 'colour' to the chord and make it want to move on strongly to the chord that follows.

In *Let's dance,* notice how the chord of C7 builds up one note at a time during the link/coda section of the song.

Let's dance link bars

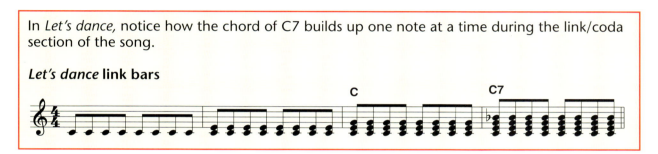

Chord parts

Easy chord part

Alternative backing part (using root position and inversions)

Not all the chords in the backing part below are in **root position**. When the three notes of the chord are arranged with the **root** (first note of the chord) like this:

they are in root position. But the three notes can be arranged in any order (called **inversions**) so that they sound better and are more comfortable to play. This is what happens in *Let's dance*.

The inversions used in *Let's dance* put the fifth of the chord on the bottom:

Chord part

Bass part

The bass part mainly uses a riff based on the notes of each chord:

Percussion parts

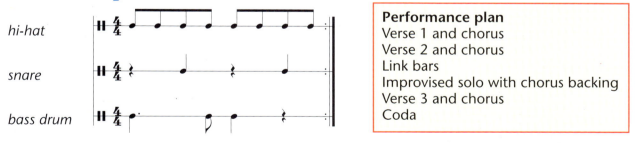

Performance plan
Verse 1 and chorus
Verse 2 and chorus
Link bars
Improvised solo with chorus backing
Verse 3 and chorus
Coda

Improvising using the blues scale

The section 'Improvised solo with chorus backing' should be treated as an instrumental section. A soloist should improvise a solo during the twelve-bar chorus section using the notes from the **blues scale** below. The blues scale is often used for improvising in jazz and rock music.

C E♭ F (F♯) G B♭

Composing melodies from chords

Root, 3rd, 5th?	5	3		3	5		5 5 5	
Melody notes:	G	A		A	G		G G G	
Words:	Let's dance,			Let's dance,			We'll do the	
Chords:	C	F / / /	F / / /	C / / /	C / /	/		

Root, 3rd, 5th?	3	3	3	3	3	3	3 3 3	
Melody notes:	B	B	B	B	B	B	A A A	
Words:	twist, the stomp, the mashed po-ta-to too,							
Chords:	G	/	/	/			F / / /	

Root, 3rd, 5th?	3 3	3 3		3	3	3	3 3 3 3	5
Melody notes:	B B	B B		B	B	A	A A A A	G
Words:	A-ny old dance that		you	want to do		but	let's dance,	
Chords:	G	/	/	/	F	/	/	/	C / / / C / / /

An important skill when writing music is being able to compose a melody from chords. Once a chord sequence has been composed, experienced songwriters find it easy to improvise a melody by ear. Less experienced composers need guidelines to begin composing a melody from chords.

First look at the chorus melody of *Let's dance* in the box above. Working in pairs one person should play the melody notes (and sing if you can) whilst the other person plays the chords.

Second, notice that the chorus melody comes from the notes of the backing chords underneath. (Remember that a chord is made up of a root – the note it is built on – a third, and a fifth.)

Look at each melody note. Notice that only the 3rd or the 5th of the chord has been used (shown on the line above the melody notes 3rd = 3, 5th = 5).

Finally make up your own variation of the chorus melody. First copy out the box below leaving plenty of space. Next, replace each missing note with a different note from the chord underneath. (NB check carefully in the box above to make sure that you have chosen a *different* melody note from the one above.) Write a replacement note above each syllable. Remember: 'po-ta-to' needs three notes because it has three syllables (one is already done for you).

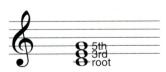

Melody notes:	G	A		A	G		....	
Words:	Let's dance,			Let's dance,			We'll do the	
Chords:	C	F / / /	F / / /	C / / /	C / /	/		

Melody notes:	B	....		B	..... A			
Words:	twist, the stomp, the mashed po-ta-to too,						
Chords:	G	/	/	/	F / / /		

Melody notes:	B		....		A G		
Words:	A- ny old dance that you		want to do but	let's dance,		
Chords:	G	/	/	/	F	/	/	/	C / / / C / / /

Music and dance in the 1950s

The 1950s and early 1960s was the era of rock 'n' roll music. Many people would say it began in New York on 12 April 1954 when Bill Haley and the Comets recorded *Rock around the clock* featuring the exciting new amplified electric guitar. Haley's music was a mixture of popular styles, especially rhythm and blues with country and western. It was a brash new sound and possessed an energy and drive particularly appealing to young people.

New rock 'n' roll stars included Elvis Presley, Little Richard, Chuck Berry and Buddy Holly. It was their music that laid foundations for the pop music of today.

For the first time the mass media (press, radio and television) promoted the new music on a world-wide scale. Every teenage coffee bar had its own juke box playing the most popular singles at full volume, and small portable record players allowed young people to play their own music freely. The record industry found a new market in teenagers hungry for popular music, and records sold in their millions.

Rock 'n' roll music revolutionized dance styles. Throughout America, new dances such as the jive and hand jive, the twist, the turn and the mashed potato became popular. They spread quickly to Britain.

In the 1950s a new teenage culture was born with rock 'n' roll stars leading the fashions of the time. Young people had much more independence and their taste in clothes, entertainment, music and lifestyle no longer reflected that of their parents. With more money in their pockets and more time on their hands, they were free to enjoy themselves. All this was reflected in the music of rock 'n' roll.

Rock 'n' roll – a new style
(not all of these ingredients are always present in any one song)

- arose from a mixture of country and western with rhythm and blues

- usually uses the twelve-bar blues structure based on a repeated sequence using three chords – I, IV, V

- basic rock beat developed from jazz

- solo singer accompanied by a variety of instruments such as piano, guitar, string bass, drums, saxophone, trumpet, trombone or backing singers (amplified instruments were gradually becoming available)

- simple lyrics

- scat singing (see page 11)

- heard live in dance halls, on juke boxes in coffee bars, and on radio

- dances such as the jive and the twist

- fashions – for boys: narrow lapels on jackets and drain-pipe trousers, white socks, string ties, cow-lick hair; for girls: full ballerina-length skirts, 'waspy' belts, flat slip-on shoes, pony-tails.

1950s teenagers in a coffee bar

Listening to rock 'n' roll music

Listen to these three rock 'n' roll songs and answer the questions that follow:

A   *Tutti frutti* performed by Elvis Presley (track 1)
B   *Little bitty pretty one* performed by Frankie Lymon (track 2)
C   *Earth Angel* performed by The Penguins (track 3)

1   Find *one* statement from *each* of the boxes below that matches each song:

a

introduction
i   piano, bass, drums and voices
ii   guitar
iii   drums & voices
iv   solo voice

b

backing singers
i   children's choir
ii   female
iii   none
iv   male

c

singing styles
i   scat & oohs
ii   scat singing
iii   humming & wahs
iv   oohs and aahs

d

chords
i   song uses chord I throughout
ii   song uses two chords: I & V
iii   song uses three chords: I, IV, V
iv   song uses more than three chords

Elvis Presley

2   From this list, write down *all* the instruments used in each song:
piano, bass, saxophones, drums, electric guitar, trumpet, trombone

Rock 'n' roll dancing

3   From this list, write down *one* feature in each song:
i   bass and backing singers repeat riffs during verses
ii   improvised electric guitar solo
iii   instruments play a short single chord between vocal lines
iv   solo verses alternate with a chorus of backing singers and instruments
v   voices sing in thirds
vi   no backing singers

Fans at a rock 'n' roll concert

I, VI, IV (II), V scat!

Scat singing is a type of jazz singing where nonsense syllables and other wordless effects are used. Ella Fitgerald was a famous singer of scat.

Try some scat singing yourselves! Learn each part separately and repeat it until you are secure, then gradually build up into a performance. After learning the parts, add the well-known melody. Try the simple accompaniments called vamps on page 12 to support the vocal parts.

Ella Fitzgerald was a famous jazz singer

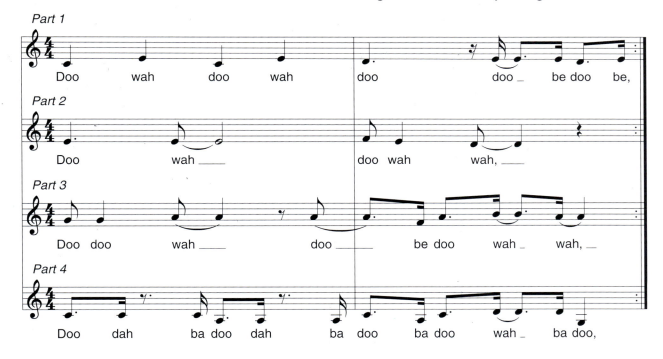

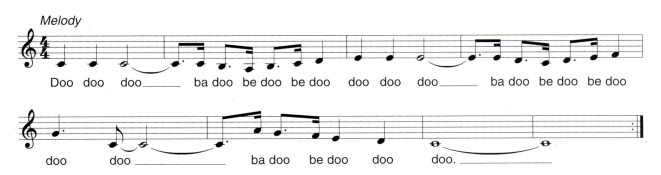

Vamps

a

I   VI   II   V

b

I   VI   II   V

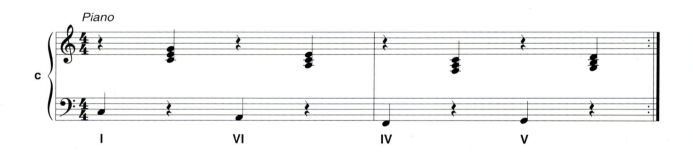

c

I   VI   IV   V

d

I   VI   IV   V

Meet chords II and VI

Revising primary chords

Remember that primary chords are the three chords in any major or minor key, which are built on the first, fourth or fifth notes of the scale. The Roman numerals I, IV and V are used to name them. These three primary chords are used more often than any other chords because between them they contain every note of the scale. This means that these three chords between them will harmonize most simple melodies satisfactorily.

Introducing chords II and VI in major keys

Two new chords used frequently in *major* keys are chords II and VI. Even though they are in a major key, chords II and VI are both *minor* chords. This means that the distance between the root and middle note of the chords is only three semitones. They are called *minor thirds* in contrast to *major thirds* which have four semitones.

Minor chords contrast with the major sounds of the three primary chords, and add variety and colour to the music.

Below are chords I, II, IV, V and VI in the key of C major.

Note: Remember, chords are named in different ways:

- *by letter name, e.g. C, A, B♭ etc.*
- *by type, e.g. D major (D), E minor (Em), 7th (C7) etc.*
- *by the Roman numeral of the scale-note on which they are built, e.g. I, IV, V etc.*

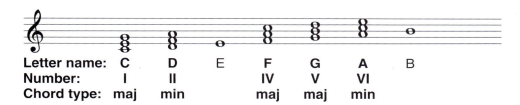

Letter name:	C	D	E	F	G	A	B
Number:	I	II		IV	V	VI	
Chord type:	maj	min		maj	maj	min	

Introducing three-chord clichés

Some chord changes or progressions are used more than others. When a particular pattern of chords is used over and over it becomes a **cliché**. Sometimes it is called a stock chord progression.

Learn to play the following clichés or stock chord progressions in the key of C:

a	Number:	I / VI / IV / V /
	Chord name and type:	C Am F G
b	Number:	I / VI / II / V /
	Chord name and type:	C Am Dm G
c	Number:	I / IV / II / V /
	Chord name and type:	C F Dm G

Earth Angel

Curtis Williams arr. CH

Perform the 1950s song *Earth Angel* by Curtis Williams (track 3). Extra scat-sung backing parts are on the page opposite. You could play one of the I, VI, IV, V vamps on page 12 to back it up.

The melody line of *Earth Angel* is made up of chord notes with some passing and auxiliary notes.

Passing notes smooth out leaps in melodies. Passing notes move in steps between chord notes:

Chord of C

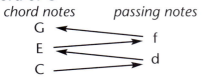

Auxiliary notes move by step to the note above or below a chord note but then return immediately to the same note:

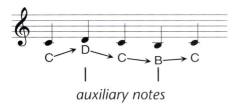

auxiliary notes

Things to do

a   In your books copy out the chord of C with its passing notes on the left. Next work out and write down the chord notes and passing notes for the chords of Am, F and G.

b   Look closely at the opening section (inside the repeat signs) of part 1 of *Earth Angel*. How many passing notes can you find?

c   Look closely at the melody line and chords of the second section of *Earth Angel*. How many auxiliary notes can you find?

Backing parts for you to try

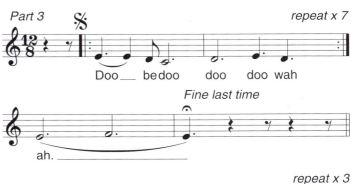

Using chords in songs

Accompaniments and backings

Once you have composed a melody for a song, and an accompanying chord sequence for the backing, it is time to think further about what type of backing or accompaniment would be most suitable. The accompaniment contributes a great deal to the mood and effect of a song, so it is important to consider it carefully.

Now listen to two traditional folk songs, arranged by Benjamin Britten, where the accompaniment 'colours' the stories most effectively. Think about the ways in which the piano shows the characters of first the plough boy, and then of the king coming upon a young woman asleep under the tree. Some of the words are printed for you to follow.

The plough boy (track 5)

This describes the thoughts of a plough boy as he dreams of rising to become a very grand and important man. He's not too bothered about cheating and lying his way to the top provided people forget his humble beginnings and treat him as someone important. But listen to how the accompaniment gets its own back, and reminds the listener of the plough boy's humble background by repeating the little tune he once used to whistle.

Notice also the way the repeated chords are bounced along to show the plough boy's energy.

A traditional plough boy leading the horses

1   A flaxen-headed cowboy as simple as
      can be
    And next a merry plough boy, I whistle o'er
      the lea.
    But now a saucy footman, I strut in worsted
      lace
    And soon I'll be a butler and whey my jolly
      face*.
    When steward I'm promoted I'll slit the
      tradesman's bill,
    My master's coffers empty my pockets for
      to fill.
    When lolling in my chariot so great a man
      I'll be,
    So great a man, so great a man, so great a
      man I'll be.
    You'll forget the little plough boy who
      whistled o'er the lea,
    You'll forget the little plough boy who
      whistled o'er the lea. (cont.)

*   *a whey-faced person was pale through
    living indoors*

The king has gone a-hunting
(track 6)

This song describes a meeting between a king out hunting and a girl he disturbs under a tree who is engaged to someone else. Listen to how the music describes the hunting horn, the galloping horse and the sleepy maiden.

1   The king has gone a-hunting beneath the
      greenwood tree,
    Beneath the greenwood tree, my
      adorable maiden,
    Beneath the greenwood tree, sweet
      maiden Marie.

2   He's got no bird a-hunting, no pigeon
      catcheth he,
    No pigeon catcheth he, my adorable
      maiden,
    No pigeon catcheth he, sweet maiden
      Marie. (cont.)

Considering chord patterns

Arranging chords into patterns is one of the most effective ways to enhance the mood of a song. Now listen to five pieces, each of which uses a different chord pattern in its accompaniment. Answer the questions as you listen. Write the answers in your books not on this page!

1   For each piece in the box below identify the type of chord pattern used in the accompaniment by matching it with its graphic in the opposite column.

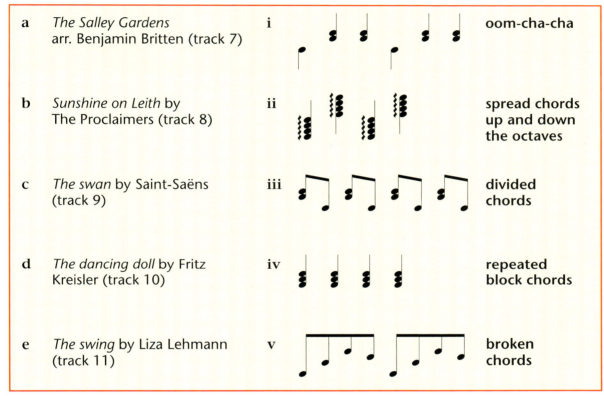

a	*The Salley Gardens* arr. Benjamin Britten (track 7)	**i**		oom-cha-cha
b	*Sunshine on Leith* by The Proclaimers (track 8)	**ii**		spread chords up and down the octaves
c	*The swan* by Saint-Saëns (track 9)	**iii**		divided chords
d	*The dancing doll* by Fritz Kreisler (track 10)	**iv**		repeated block chords
e	*The swing* by Liza Lehmann (track 11)	**v**		broken chords

2   **a**   Which piece is *not* accompanied by the acoustic piano?
     b   Which instrument accompanies this piece?

3   **a**   Which piece might be equally well accompanied by the harp?
     b   Why do you think this?

4   Choose *two* of the five pieces. Write about the way in which the chord pattern used in each accompaniment made the piece particularly effective. Don't forget to say which piece you are discussing, what chord pattern its accompaniment uses, as well as discussing how effective it is.

Benjamin Britten (composer and accompanist) and Peter Pears (tenor) discuss a performance

Performing chord patterns

There are many ways of performing chordal backings apart from just playing block chords. Four different ways of making patterns with chords are given below. Practise each one until you can play it comfortably.

Note: Chord fingerings for both hands on a full-sized keyboard are given. However, these chords may also be played using two hands. If performed on pitched percussion instruments, one beater could be held in the left hand, and one or two beaters in the right. The patterns should then be divided between the two hands.

Luciano Pavarotti rehearsing with his accompanist

a Block chords using the chord of C

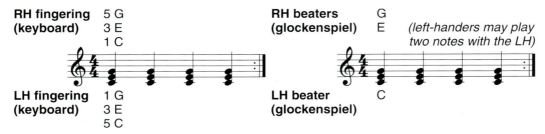

RH fingering 5 G
(keyboard) 3 E
1 C

LH fingering 1 G
(keyboard) 3 E
5 C

RH beaters G
(glockenspiel) E *(left-handers may play two notes with the LH)*

LH beater C
(glockenspiel)

b Oom-cha-cha-cha chords using the chord of C

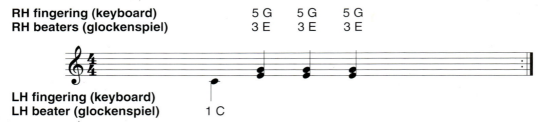

RH fingering (keyboard) 5 G 5 G 5 G
RH beaters (glockenspiel) 3 E 3 E 3 E

LH fingering (keyboard)
LH beater (glockenspiel) 1 C

c Broken chords using the chord of C

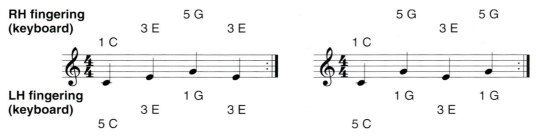

RH fingering 5 G
(keyboard) 3 E 3 E 1 C
1 C

LH fingering 1 G
(keyboard) 3 E 3 E
5 C

Glockenspiel players should play C with the left beater, G with the right beater, and E with either beater.

d   Divided chords using the chord of C

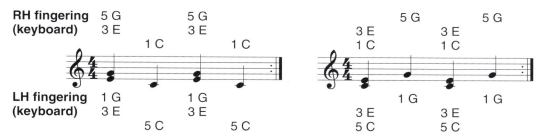

For these patterns, fingerings 2 and 4 may be easier than 3 and 5.
Glockenspiel players should play C with the left beater, G and E with the right beater.

Now play through each pattern again, this time using the following chord sequence. Each pattern is worth four beats, so you will need to change chord at the beginning of every pattern:

C / / / F / / / G / / / Am / / / Dm / / / F / / / G / / / C / / /

Noel Gallagher from 'Oasis' working with composer Burt Bacharach

Listening to O holy night

Listen to *O holy night* (track 12), especially to the backing or accompaniment. Notice the rippling **broken chords** which give a flowing effect especially suitable for a gentle song like this.

Now look at the section from the **score** below. Notice how the accompaniment is made up from the notes of a series of chords. Notice, too, that there are only one or two chords per bar. Breaking the notes of the chords up like this keeps the movement going throughout, and helps create the gentle mood of the song.

a See how the notes in the right hand of the piano part are created from the notes of the chords in each bar. Look at each note in the piano part: first work out their names and then find them in the chord boxes underneath their bars.

b Now look at the vocal part and notice how the melody uses mainly notes from the chords below it, plus the occasional passing note. In pairs, or with your teacher, name the notes of the melody and decide whether each melody note is a chord note, a passing note, or an auxiliary note.

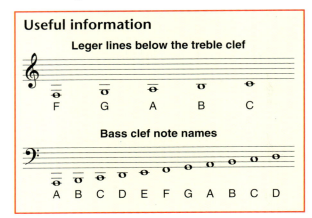

Useful information

Leger lines below the treble clef

Bass clef note names

Opening of *O holy night*

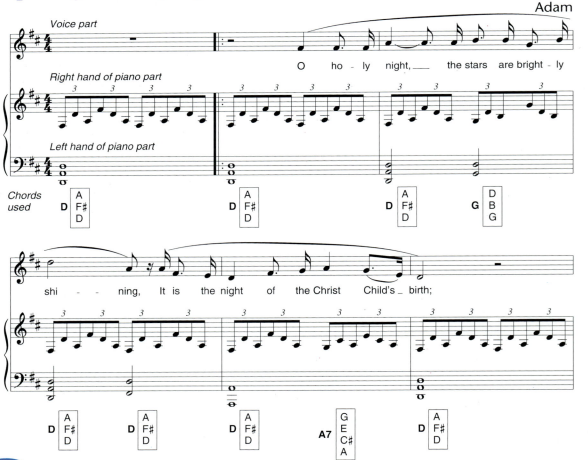

Words of *O holy night*

1 O holy night, the stars are brightly shining,
It is the night of the Christ Child's birth;
Long lay the world in sin and darkness pining,
Until He came, the One of highest worth.

A thrill of hope, the weary world rejoices,
For now there breaks a new and glorious morn,
Fall on your knees, O hear the angel voices,
O night divine, the night when Christ was born.
O night divine, for Christ was born.

Assessing accompaniments

Below are two melodies, both with chordal accompaniments. Listen carefully to each and answer the questions.

Balulalow from *A ceremony of carols* by Benjamin Britten (1913–76)

1 Listen to four different accompaniments to the words of this sixteenth century lullaby (tracks 13–16). Only one of them is right. Which is the correct accompaniment and why?

1 O my dear heart, young Je - su sweet, Pre - pare thy cra - dle in my spreit, And

I shall rock Thee to my heart,__ And ne - ver more from Thee__ de - part.

1   O my dear heart, young Jesu sweet,
    Prepare thy cradle in my spreit *(spirit)*,
    And I shall rock Thee to my heart,
    And never more from Thee depart.

2   But I shall praise Thee evermore,
    With sanges *(songs)* sweet unto Thy
       gloir *(glory)*,
    The knees of my heart shall I bow, shall I
       bow,
    And sing that right balulalow.

Das Wandern (Wandering) by Schubert (1797–1828)

2 Listen to this song (track 18). The accompaniment is as important as the words in carrying its meaning to the listener. Look at the description of what the English words mean and describe how the accompaniment brings out their meaning and emphasizes the mood of the song.

What the words mean

1   The miller sings of his joy in travelling and is sorry for those who don't feel the 'travel bug'.

2   Rivers and streams have always been an example of travelling, as they are never still.

3   Mill wheels too turn all day without stopping.

4   Even millstones, for all their weight, never stop moving.

5   The miller longs to travel forever. He asks if he can leave work so that he can gain his heart's desire.

Rondos and recurring structures

'Recurring' means returning again and again. This project is about some of the ways in which composers make pieces longer by using their first idea several times and contrasting it with new ideas in between.

Carillon

Francis Poulenc

Carillon has a typical recurring structure because it alternates a main theme (section A) with a number of other contrasting sections of music. This type of composition structure, where the main theme is alternated with several contrasting sections, is called a **rondo**. You will learn more about rondos on page 25.

Performance plan

This piece may be performed in a number of ways to suit the time available:
Section A and Section A/Coda should be performed *tutti* (everyone).
Sections B, C, D and E should be performed by smaller groups.

Complete performance plan

A   B   A   C   A   D   A   E   A   B   D   A/Coda

Shortened performance plan

A   B   A   C   A/Coda

A carillon is a set of at least 23 carillon bells hung in a tower and operated from a keyboard of wooden levers played by a half-closed fist. In addition, the larger bells are connected to foot pedals. Tunes for a carillon need to be carefully chosen as the sound of a bell carries on ringing until the vibrations die away naturally, and there is no way to stop or alter its sound once it has been struck!

Poulenc's *Carillon* comes from his *French suite* and was originally composed for wind instruments, side drum and piano. However, the style would suit a carillon well – since the music is built on very few chords, there would be no clashes of harmony as the bells continued to sound.

Carillon, Wellington, New Zealand

Carillon

Francis Poulenc arr. CH

More about musical structure

All music has a **structure** or **form**. The structure is the way in which the music is put together to make a satisfying piece. A piece which is not well structured sounds as if it is 'lost' and doesn't know where it is going. A good structure will use a mix of familiar and new material – **repetition** and **contrast**.

Repetition is an important ingredient in all styles of music. Repetition is used to remind the listener of important musical ideas from time to time, so that they don't lose the thread of the music.

Now think of the melodies that you have composed and the way in which you went about composing them. First, you experimented until you found a good idea. Next, you wanted to make your piece longer. One way of making the piece longer was to repeat the first idea. But how many times could you repeat your idea before the music began to lose interest? Once, twice, three, four times? Whatever your decision, at some point your composition needed **contrast**. New, fresh, contrasting ideas keep the music alive, and are also necessary to keep the interest going.

> Remember: repetition and contrast give longer pieces of music structure or form. The right balance of repetition and contrast leads to a very satisfying piece of music.

Some structures explained

You may already have listened to, composed or performed pieces in an A B A structure or **ternary form**. Ternary form has the essential ingredients of good structure: repetition (**A**) and contrast (**B**). This makes it a very satisfying musical structure.

Another popular musical structure is where a single main idea is repeated several times with different contrasting themes in between. This structure is known as **rondo form** – see the diagram opposite.

1	Theme	A
2	New material 1	B
3	Theme	A
4	New material 2	C
5	Theme	A
6	New material 3	D
7	Theme	A
8	Coda	Coda

Another way of showing this is:

A	B	A	C	A	D	A	Coda

The contrasting ideas are called **episodes**. You can have as many different episodes as you like provided the theme is played after each one. The **coda** comes at the end and rounds off the piece.

Many songs have a similar structure where a chorus is repeated between each verse. But the **verse and chorus** structure found in songs is different from the structure of instrumental rondos. A song does not usually begin with the chorus, and each verse usually has the same melody. A rondo is different from this because it begins with the theme and each episode is different from the others.

Another style of music which frequently uses an alternating structure is jazz. In jazz, a recurring (repeated) melody is known as a chorus. The chorus is played in between contrasting solo improvisations.

Listening to Carillon

Carillon bells

Francis Poulenc (1899–1963) was one of a group of six young French composers, known as 'Les Six', who worked in Paris after World War I. Poulenc and his friends were influenced by Satie (who composed *Gymnopédie*), and wanted their music to be direct, to say what they meant instead of being 'romantic' or 'impressionist'. Poulenc composed chamber music, a number of ballets, many piano and organ pieces, and vocal music. *Carillon* is the finale to a suite of dances he composed in 1935.

Carillon was based on melodies from the sixteenth century by another French composer named Claude Gervaise. In the sixteenth century, music was written in 'easy' keys without more than one or two sharps or flats. This was because ways of making wind instruments able to play in tune in every key had not yet been developed, and most could only play in tune in a few simple keys. Even though Poulenc wrote the piece for modern instruments, *Carillon* is all in the key of C and there are no **accidentals** (sharps and flats). It is also very suitable for a carillon to play.

Now, listen to *Carillon* (track 19) and follow the single line score on page 27. Remember that the sign below means **repeat**. You must look out for repeat signs, and follow the music inside them *twice*.

‖: (repeat all the music between these signs) :‖

Next, write the answers to these questions on the answer sheet:

1   In this piece Poulenc uses different instruments in each section of *Carillon* to bring out the contrasts between the melodies and also between the repeats. Which instruments are heard in the **A** sections, and where does the side drum play?

2   Apart from the different instruments used, describe another way in which the sections are contrasted.

3   A carillon is often placed in a tall stone tower so it can be seen and heard by a large number of people. Suppose a carillon were to be built in your town:
   a   in what sort of area should it be sited?
   b   on what sort of occasions might it be played?

4   Give three features which you would expect to find in music suitable for playing on a carillon.

5   Now discuss with your teacher some of the differences between a carillon and a ring of bells. What is a ring of bells? Where might you expect to hear and see a carillon? (Listen to track 20.)

Playing a carillon

Carillon

Francis Poulenc arr. CH

Happy hour

Lloyd Scott

Happy hour, composed by Lloyd Scott, is a piece of **trad** (traditional) **jazz** from the 1920s. Jazz was the most popular form of music in America and Europe at that time. Hundreds of jazz bands flourished, particularly in the American cities of New Orleans, New York and Chicago, where many black musicians lived.

Improvisation is the most important feature of all jazz styles and this made performers like Louis Armstrong, Bix Beiderbecke and Benny Goodman the musical superstars of their time. Popular songs were recycled and performed by almost every jazz band, each adding their own particular style to other composers' music. Hundreds of new jazz melodies were also composed and these became the 'standards' of the jazz repertoire. The alternation of well-known **choruses** and improvised **solos** was a winning formula, and made jazz one of the most important styles of music of the twentieth century.

Learn the chorus of *Happy hour* above and perform it before listening to the whole piece. This is an unusual jazz chorus because it is so short.

Listening to *Happy hour*
(track 21)

Now listen to *Happy hour* (track 21) and answer the following questions. Do not write the answers here. Use your books or a separate sheet of paper.

1 *Happy hour* divides into eleven sections of music which are listed in the left-hand column of the box opposite. In the right-hand column are eleven descriptions of the music. Match each section with its correct musical description, and connect each pair by drawing a line between them, as in the example given.

section 1	chorus twice
section 2	chorus twice
section 3	chorus
section 4	chorus twice with banjo break
section 5	trombone solo
section 6	clarinet duet
section 7	introduction
section 8	baritone saxophone solo
section 9	clarinet solo
section 10	mixed instrumental ensemble
section 11	saxophone duet

2 True or false? For every statement below about *Happy hour*, say whether it is *true* or *false*.

i All sections of the orchestra are heard in *Happy hour*.

ii Performers make up their solos as they play them.

iii There is always at least one instrument keeping a steady beat.

iv *Happy hour* has three beats in the bar.

v There is no syncopation in *Happy hour*.

3 Like a lot of jazz pieces, *Happy hour* is based on the same melody (the chorus) repeated many times. What features in the music hold the listener's interest right to the end of the piece even though there are so many repetitions?

Ritorno

CH with thanks to Messiaen

1   Perform *Ritorno* printed below as a class or group.

E E D C A G   C   A A G   E   D E

E E D C A G   A   D E G E G A C A

Coda

D   E   G   E   G   A C   A

2   Learn the notes of the minor pentatonic scale below as a class or group. Then work individually to try out one or two improvisations each lasting the same length as the *Ritorno* above (eight bars). You may like to use its question and answer structure in your own improvisations. You may also want to use the same rhythm, but as you gain confidence, try to invent your own rhythm to fit in with the style.

3   With your teacher or group work out a performance plan. Decide how many repetitions of the *Ritorno* and how many solos should be played to make the piece most effective.

4   Begin with the *Ritorno.* After each repetition perform an eight-bar *solo* improvisation using the notes of the minor pentatonic scale (see below). End with the *Ritorno* followed by the Coda.

Minor pentatonic scale for solo improvisations

A   C   D   E   G   A

A jazz combo in New Orleans

Gaudete

This early carol was written in Latin which was the official language of the Christian Church until the Reformation in the sixteenth century. Latin is a very easy language to sing, and so you should enjoy singing this carol in its original language. The translation is: 'Rejoice! Christ is born of the Virgin Mary.'

As in many medieval carols the verses are in English to make the meaning of the words clear.

gaudete is pronounced 'gow-dey-tey', and means 'rejoice'.

Traditional arr. CH
English words MM

Listening to a rondo

Horn concerto no. 4 in E♭ by W.A. Mozart

A concerto is a piece of music written for a solo instrument and an orchestra. The solo part is an opportunity for performers to display their skill, and is frequently very difficult.

Concertos usually have three movements: the first is often quite fast with two main themes; the second movement is slow and song-like (lyrical); the third is usually fast and jolly and often in the form of a **rondo**. The finale (last movement) of Mozart's fourth *Horn concerto in E♭* is an example of a rondo.

Listen carefully to this piece (track 22) and notice its structure. How many main melodies does it have? Use **A**, **B, C** etc to name each melody. Below are a number of different melody plans. Which plan best matches the form of this rondo?

```
1  A  B  A  C  A
2  A  B  A  C  A  D  A  E  A
3  A  B  A  C  A  B  A
4  A  B  C  B  A
```

On page 32 there is a plan to help you follow the structure of Mozart's rondo as you listen. With a bit of practice you should be able to understand a little more of how the composer used three melody ideas to make a whole movement. First, you need to be thoroughly familiar with the three melodies. Listen to them a number of times or, better still, play them yourself until you really know them.

Playing the French horn

A soloist playing a trumpet concerto in the European Music for Youth Prize

31

Rondo plan

Read along each section of the chart as you listen to the music.

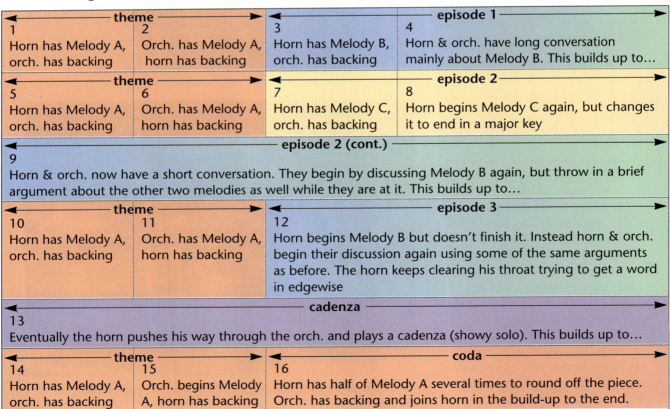

theme		episode 1	
1 Horn has Melody A, orch. has backing	**2** Orch. has Melody A, horn has backing	**3** Horn has Melody B, orch. has backing	**4** Horn & orch. have long conversation mainly about Melody B. This builds up to…

theme		episode 2	
5 Horn has Melody A, orch. has backing	**6** Orch. has Melody A, horn has backing	**7** Horn has Melody C, orch. has backing	**8** Horn begins Melody C again, but changes it to end in a major key

episode 2 (cont.)
9 Horn & orch. now have a short conversation. They begin by discussing Melody B again, but throw in a brief argument about the other two melodies as well while they are at it. This builds up to…

theme		episode 3
10 Horn has Melody A, orch. has backing	**11** Orch. has Melody A, horn has backing	**12** Horn begins Melody B but doesn't finish it. Instead horn & orch. begin their discussion again using some of the same arguments as before. The horn keeps clearing his throat trying to get a word in edgewise

cadenza
13 Eventually the horn pushes his way through the orch. and plays a cadenza (showy solo). This builds up to…

theme		coda
14 Horn has Melody A, orch. has backing	**15** Orch. begins Melody A, horn has backing	**16** Horn has half of Melody A several times to round off the piece. Orch. has backing and joins horn in the build-up to the end.

$\frac{6}{8}$ *and compound time*

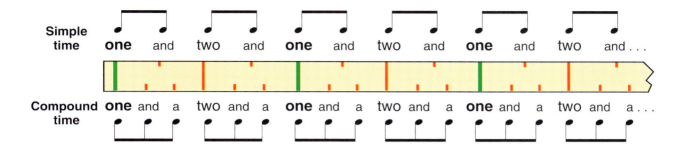

Listen to an excerpt from Holst's *Suite no 2 in F major for military band* (track 23). You will hear a march with two beats in a bar. There are two quite different sections. The second section changes to a minor key and begins after a loud chord played by the whole band, so you should be able to hear where it begins quite easily.

As you listen to the excerpt, tap the beat quietly on your knee with your index finger. See if you can discover whether the pulse of the second section remains the same as the first, or whether it becomes faster or slower. What else do you notice about the minor section?

Although both sections of Holst's march have two beats in a bar, the first section is in **simple time** whilst the second section is in **compound time**.

In the diagram above you can see the difference in the rhythm of the two sections. In the first section the beat divides into halves and if you are very quick you might be able to count 'one and two and' in time with the music. In the second section the beat divides into threes and you can count 'one and a two and a' as the music plays. Although compound time does not come from marching but from dancing, it is often used in marches to add lightness to the rhythm.

- If the beat can be divided evenly into two, the piece is in **simple time.**
- If the beat can be divided evenly into three, the piece is in **compound time.**

Revising pulse and time

Before you learn more about compound time you should revise what you know about time so far. We all know what a beat is. In music, **beat** and **pulse** mean the same thing. We all understand what 'keeping a steady beat' means.

Keeping a steady beat is most important when people are moving to music. It keeps them moving all together at the same time. Otherwise they would get out of step. Two types of music where keeping a steady beat is particularly important are shown here:

March									
Count:	1	2	3	4	=	4 beats	*Left*	*Right*	*Left*	*Right*

Waltz								
Count:	1	2	3		=	3 beats	*Oom* – pah – pah	

The first beat in each group is the most important and is emphasized in performance. On the stave, groups of beats are separated by barlines.

Bars and barlines

A **bar** is a small section of music which contains a particular number of beats.
A **barline** shows the end of a bar. A **double barline** shows the end of the piece.

bar ← → barline ← → barline ← bar → double barline

Remember:

• In a **march** there are **2** or **4 beats** in a bar.
• In a **waltz** there are **3 beats** in a bar.

Revising time signatures

A **time signature** shows the number of beats in a bar. A time signature is two numbers placed one above the other at the beginning of a piece of music.

The **top number** tells us how many beats there are in each bar; the **bottom number** tells us what sort of beat to count. A piece with crotchet beats has 4 on the bottom line of its time signature. Minim beats have 2 on the bottom. Quaver beats have 8 on the bottom. Most of your pieces so far have had crotchet beats. Crotchet beats are the most common.

Waltzing at a court ball at the Hofburg, 1900

2 crotchet beats	3 crotchet beats	4 crotchet beats	3 quaver beats	2 minin beats
$\frac{2}{4}$	$\frac{3}{4}$	$\frac{4}{4}$	$\frac{3}{8}$	$\frac{2}{2}$

Pieces with 2, 3 or 4 on the top line of their time signatures are said to be in **simple time**.

Learning about compound time

We have learned that in compound time the beat divides evenly into three. This means that in compound time the beat will need to be a **dotted note** because dotted notes can be divided evenly into three.

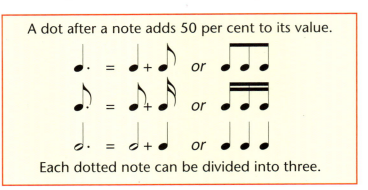

A dot after a note adds 50 per cent to its value.

Each dotted note can be divided into three.

Learning about 6/8 time

An example of compound time is 6/8. 6/8 has two dotted crochet beats in each bar.

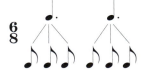

To help you remember:

Simple time = ordinary beats (e.g. crotchets)

2/4 time has 2 crotchet beats per bar (4 on the bottom line means crotchet beats)

Compound time = dotted beats (e.g. dotted crotchets)

Remember, in 6/8 time:

- there are *only 2* beats in every bar
- the 2 beats are dotted beats
- there are 3 quavers to each beat.

Simple time (e.g. 2/4):

count: 1 and 2 and   1 and 2 and

Compound time (e.g. 6/8):

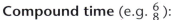

count: 1- and- a - 2- and- a   1-and- a   2- and- a

Military marching band

Using compound time: performing The dargason

Compound time is used in a great many traditional dance styles from Ireland and the British Isles. *The dargason* is a traditional English folk dance melody from the sixteenth century. It has the typical characteristics of a jig (a lively dance with a skipping movement) and a time signature of $\frac{6}{8}$. Remember, in $\frac{6}{8}$ time there are two beats in each bar and each of these beats divides evenly into three.

Perform this arrangement of *The dargason* together as a class. The first stage is to clap the rhythm together with your teacher to get the feel of compound time. Make sure you can do this with confidence before you tackle *The dargason*.

The dargason

Traditional arr. CH

Instrumental melody 1

G E C C C E F G F E F D D D F G A G F

E C C C C C B A G F D D D D C B A G

Instrumental melody 2

G E C C C E F G F E F D D D F G A G F

E C C C E F G F E F D D D F G A G F

Instrumental melody 3

G E C C C C C B A G F D D D D C B A G

E C C C C C B A G F D D D D C B A G

Counter-melody

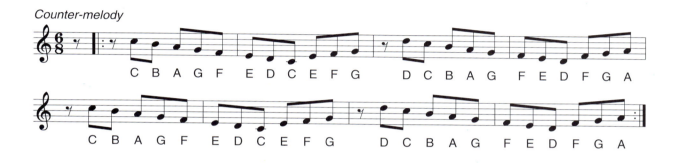

C B A G F E D C E F G D C B A G F E D F G A

C B A G F E D C E F G D C B A G F E D F G A

Bass 1

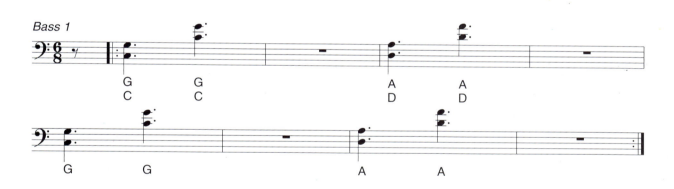

G G A A
C C D D

G G A A

Bass 2

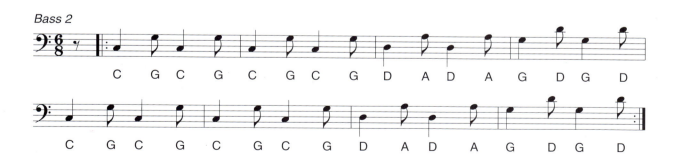

C G C G C G C G D A D A G D G D

C G C G C G C G D A D A G D G D

Some traditional Celtic instruments

The traditional music of Ireland, Wales, and from parts of Scotland and England, all comes from the same ancient Celtic tradition. Likenesses can be found in the types of songs, dances, rhythms, melodies and instruments. Irish traditional music in particular is deeply rooted in ancient Celtic music and still plays an important role in the daily life of its people. Traditional songs and dances are performed at social gatherings such as ceilidhs, in meeting places such as bars and taverns, and for many community events and special occasions such as weddings, festivals and fairs.

Music festivals are popular throughout the British Isles, and great value is placed on instrumental skills, singing, and dancing.

Songs and dances are learned from other performers, and each performer constantly updates old music with modern influences or musical ideas from other cultures. The recently popular dance show 'Riverdance' is a good example of the way in which traditional and pop music can combine to produce something new and vibrant. At the bottom of the page are some of the traditional instruments which may vary from one country to another.

The listening exercise on page 39 opposite includes six excerpts of Irish dance music. In the box below is the name of each dance you will hear, and the instrument(s) playing the backing.

Name of dance	Backing instrument(s)
Down the lane (track 24)	guitar
Brian O'Lynn (track 25)	drone played by pipes
Seán sa cheo (track 26)	guitar and bodhrán
The old bridge (track 27)	guitar and double bass
The Danish quadrille (track 28)	guitar and mandolin
The battering ram (track 29)	bodhrán

The photos shown are some of the less well-known instruments used in the six dances for both the melody and the backing.

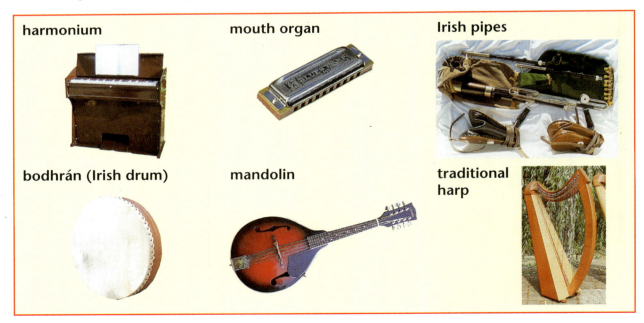

harmonium

mouth organ

Irish pipes

bodhrán (Irish drum)

mandolin

traditional harp

Listening to traditional Irish music

Listen to six traditional Irish dances and answer the questions as you listen. Write the answers in your books.

A *Down the lane* **B** *Brian O'Lynn*

C *Seán sa cheo* **D** *The old bridge*

E *The Danish quadrille* **F** *The battering ram*

1 Which instrument or instruments plays the *melody* in each of these pieces? Choose from:

fiddle flute harp guitar pipes trumpet mouth organ harmonium bodhrán mandolin accordion double bass

2 Give the correct time signature for each dance. Choose from:

i $\frac{6}{8}$ (a jig)

ii $\frac{3}{4}$ (a waltz)

iii $\frac{2}{4}$ (a reel)

An Irish ceilidh

3 You already know the structures ABA, AB, and AABA. Below are the structure patterns used in these dances. Match the correct structure with each dance.

Note: You may use the same answer more than once.

i AABB
ii AA
iii AABBA
iv ABCA

For discussion:

4 Many young people in western countries do not know anything about their own folk songs and dances because they are hardly ever seen or heard.

i Does it matter if young people do not know the traditional folk songs and dances of their own country?

ii Do you think folk songs and dances should be taught in schools so that they don't die out?

iii If you think they should be taught in schools, which subject should they come under?

Folk dancing

Performing Suffolk morris

Doreen Carwithen arr. CH

Perform *Suffolk morris* by Doreen Carwithen, choosing instruments with a folk-type sound as far as possible.

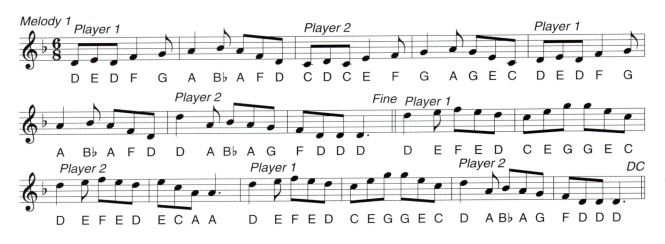

Melody 1

Player 1 — D E D F · G A Bb A F D · C D C E · F G A G E C · D E D F · G

Player 2 — A Bb A F D · D A Bb A G · F D D D · Fine

Player 1 — D E F E D · C E G G E C

Player 2 — D E F E D · E C A A · Player 1 D E F E D · C E G G E C · Player 2 D A Bb A G · F D D D · DC

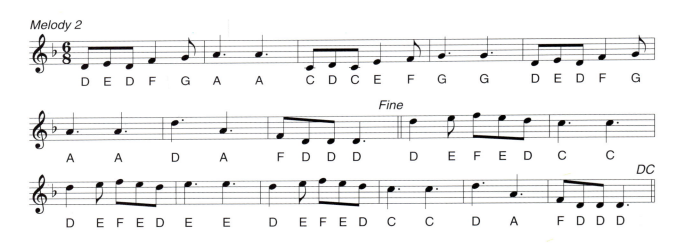

Melody 2

D E D F · G A A · C D C E · F G G · D E D F · G
A A · D A · F D D D · Fine D E F E D · C C
D E F E D · E E · D E F E D · C C · D A · F D D D · DC

Counter-melody

D E F G A · C D E F G · D E F G A · D A F D D D · Fine · DC

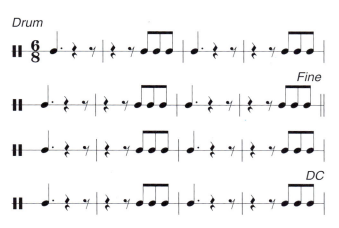

English morris dancing

Listening to Suffolk morris

Phrase 1

Phrase 2

Listen to *Suffolk morris* (track 30) by Doreen Carwithen, who was born in 1922. This piece was originally written for the Framlingham College Orchestra in Suffolk to perform when royalty visited the school. *Suffolk morris* is the third of a set of four pieces called *Suffolk suite*. Doreen Carwithen, an experienced composer of music for film and TV, describes her piece in the following way:

> '*The dancers, wearing traditional costumes decorated with ribbons and bells, begin a lively dance. A brief slower section allows them to get their breath back before the dance rhythm returns, and off they go again, through the market square and down the high street.*'

The opening section of *Suffolk morris* divides into two eight-bar phrases. Follow these two phrases printed above, and answer the questions.

1   *Suffolk morris* is in $\frac{6}{8}$ time:

    a   Is $\frac{6}{8}$ time a simple time or a compound time?

    b   How many beats in the bar are there in $\frac{6}{8}$ time?

2   *Suffolk morris* divides into three sections overall. Which of the following describes the shape of the whole piece?

    i   A B C
    ii   A B A
   iii A B B
   iv A A B

3   The first section of *Suffolk morris* uses phrases 1 and 2 only. Write the order in which these phrases appear. The beginning has been completed for you.

1	2	1					

4   The second section of *Suffolk morris* contrasts with the first and third. Using the following headings, write a short description of the changes that take place in the music in the second section:

    time signature   **dynamics**

        tempo   **texture**

    use of instruments   **mood**

Looking at how composers work

The main features of the first section of *Suffolk morris* are:

1   Use of the **aeolian mode**. This ancient mode was used a great deal in traditional music. It is similar to the minor scale but the seventh note is different, e.g. C instead of C#.

aeolian mode

D   E   F   G   A   B♭   C   D

2   A sixteen-bar melody in $\frac{6}{8}$ time made up of two eight-bar sections.

- the first section of the melody (**A**) uses a two-bar **motif** (idea) played three times. The second time it is heard a tone lower, making it a **sequence**. Finally, there is a two-bar **rounding off** phrase.

- the second section of the melody (**B**) is made up of two question-and-answer phrases. The second answer here is the same as the rounding off phrase in section A.

3   The piece uses only three chords **I** (Dm), **V** (Am) and **VII** (C):

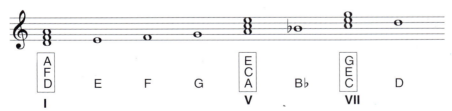

4   The piece uses sustained (held on) bass notes, or a bass riff using the root and fifth of each chord.

5   There is a percussion backing.

These simple features can be used by anyone composing music. Listen to *Suffolk morris* again, and notice particularly the way the composer has used these features in this piece.

Listening to more music in compound time

Listen to four contrasting pieces of music. Each piece is in $\frac{6}{8}$ time. The four pieces are called:

1   *Canarios* by Gaspar Sanz (track 31)
2   *Shepherd's song* from *Symphony no 6* by Beethoven (track 32)
3   *E. l mare e. l pare* traditional (track 33)
4   *Fantasia on the dargason* by Holst (track 34)

Now answer these questions in your book:

1   Write down the title of each piece. Look at the statements in the box below. By the side of each title, write *one* correct statement chosen from **a – d**, *one* from **e – h**, and *one* from **i – l**, i.e. *three* statements in total.

Instruments	Layers	Pulse rate
a military band	**e** melody heard first on violins	**i** the second fastest
b symphony orchestra	**f** many layers, counter-melody is *Greensleeves*	**j** the second slowest
c solo guitar	**g** melody, strummed chords and drum rhythms	**k** the fastest
d medieval instruments	**h** melody and bass notes only	**l** the slowest

2   Choose *one* of the four pieces. Write down its title, then comment on three features *other than those listed above* that you have noticed about this piece.

3   Which one of the four pieces do you think is the *least* suitable for dancing? Write down reasons for your choice.

Medieval musicians

Textures and timbres in the music of Japan

A Japanese score of *Etenraku* for hichiriki.

Listening to new sounds

Texture and **timbre** are important elements in the music of Japan. Instrumental timbres are carefully chosen so that each layer of sound can be clearly heard in the overall texture. This gives the music a clear, uncluttered effect.

On the opposite page are three graphic scores. Each belongs to the opening of a different piece of Japanese music. Listen carefully to each piece (tracks 35–37) and do the following tasks. Write down your answers:

1 Match each piece to the correct graphic score.

2 Match each piece to one of the following descriptions of *texture*:

a a clear melody accompanied by two drone bass notes

b a monophonic texture, i.e. a single melody played by one or more instruments without accompaniment

c two of the same instruments are playing. One plays the melody. The other plays a decorated version of the same melody.

3 Match each piece to one of the Japanese instruments described below.

a The **shamisen** is a three-stringed lute. The strings are plucked by a large wooden or ivory plectrum. It has a square sound-box which is traditionally covered with animal skin, and a long neck or finger-board.

b The **shakuhachi** is a curved open-ended bamboo flute with four finger-holes on the front and one at the back. A variety of breath sounds is created by blowing across the opening at an angle of 45 degrees.

Shakuhachi

c The **koto** is a long type of zither (a plucked instrument) whose shape is said to have come from the shape of a crouching dragon. The koto has thirteen strings which are plucked. Its sound is similar to that of the harp.

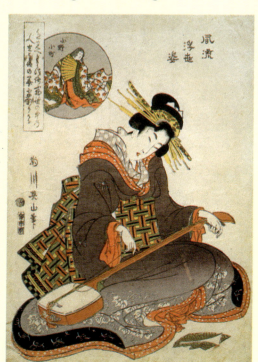

Playing the shamisen

Koto

Graphic scores

1a

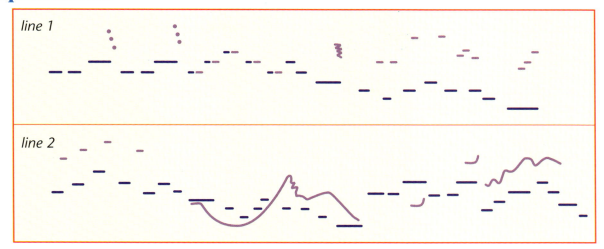

1b

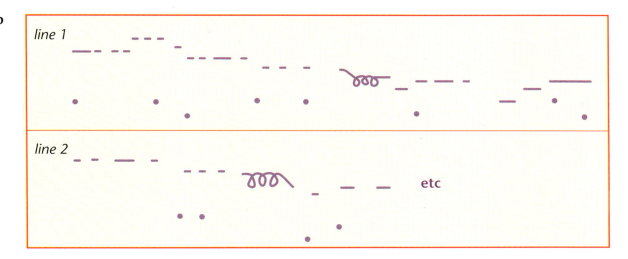

1c

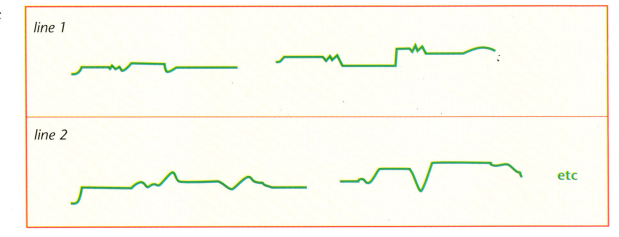

More about Japanese music

Japanese music reflects the culture and lifestyle of a very ancient nation. As in western music, in Japanese music there tends to be a distinction between art music, traditional folk music, and modern popular music. Art music and folk music are the traditional styles of Japan and can be traced back many centuries. Copies of Japanese art music have existed in notation since the eighth century so that the earliest music is still performed in the traditional style.

Kabuki performance

The most ancient music is **Gagaku**. Gagaku developed between 794–1192 AD and was originally the ceremonial court music of the most powerful nobility and upper classes. Gagaku was performed by musicians and dancers, and provided a pageant on a grand scale at court festivals or religious ceremonies held in temples.

Three other important styles of art music developed alongside drama. These are the musical accompaniments to three types of plays, Noh, Kabuki and Bunraku.

Kabuki is a more popular type of theatre. It began in the seventeenth century and was watched by all classes of people. Kabuki began as a simple dance-drama based on Buddhist folk dances of the time. It was originally accompanied by singing and a small ensemble of drums and gongs. Later, as the form developed, the dramas became longer, often lasting for a whole day, and the instrumental ensemble was made larger with the inclusion of a number of shamisens. Stories were either historical or about the merchant classes.

Noh is a type of theatre that developed between 1192–1333 AD in which music, dance and literature all play an equal part. Noh plays use no scenery and the stage area has no curtain. Any props or shapes used on stage are very symbolic and costumes lack colour, except for the main characters. The music consists of solo singing and a unison chorus accompanied by only four instruments.

Noh play

Bunraku, is a form of puppet theatre that developed in the seventeenth century, similar to Kabuki. A Bunraku performance consists of three main elements: the art of the puppeteer, the words of a narrator and singer, and the music of a shamisen player. The puppeteer moves about the stage while working the puppet. The lower part of the puppeteer's body is hidden by a high board placed at the front of the stage. The story is told in a kind of half-speaking and half-singing and is accompanied by the shamisen.

Bunraku puppet play

Japanese scales

Five and seven note scales are very common throughout the world and in all periods of musical history. Five note or **pentatonic** scales are used widely in Japanese music. There are a number of different forms of the pentatonic scale. Two contrasting pentatonic scales that are used a great deal in music for shakuhachi, koto and shamisen are the Japanese **In** and **Yo** scales. Play each of the scales below and familiarize yourself with their characteristic sounds.

The In scale
The In scale is the more widely used of the two scales. It is thought to have a 'dark' sound because it contains several semitones (marked with a slur).

E F A B D E   E C B A F E

The Yo scale
The Yo scale is thought to be 'bright' sounding. It contains no semitones.

E F# A B D E   E C# B A F# E

Note: Both scales exist in two forms, ascending and descending. The ascending form is used if a section of melody goes up whilst the descending version is used when a section of melody goes down.

Performing Sakura

Sakura is a Japanese folk song based on the In scale. *Sakura* contains several features found in much Japanese music. These are:

- the music is slow moving, gentle, and very smooth with few leaps
- the music is clear and uncluttered
- the music uses a pentatonic **In scale** containing semitones.

Sing the notes of both the ascending and descending In scale to 'lah' before you learn the song. Remember to sing different notes ascending and descending.

Now sing *Sakura* ('Cherry blossom') in its original Japanese. It is a song about the beauty of cherry blossom when the spring sky is veiled by its bloom and the air is filled with its perfume. Is it mist? Or clouds? We will have to go and see. The Japanese syllables are easy to sing and sound best, as a translation does not fit the melody very well.

Voice 1

arr. R. Mitchell

Sa – ku – ra, sa – ku – ra, ya – yo – i – no so – ra – wa

mi – wa – ta – su ka – gi – ri. Ka – su – mi – ka ku – mo – ka

ni – o – i – zo i zu – ru i – za – ya

i – za – ya mi – ni – yu – ka – ri.

Japanese musicians

Improvising using the In scale

Listen again to *Tamuke* (track 35) for solo shakuhachi, and follow its graphic score on page 47. Notice each of the following features:

- the piece has no beat or metre
- the excerpt divides into phrases of different lengths, each dictated by the length of the performer's breath
- each phrase is separated by a short silence
- often phrases begin with a sliding up to a long note and end with a long note
- the whole piece (not all of it is included in the excerpt) gets gradually higher in pitch and then lower, rather like a mountain shape
- the excerpt begins very slowly and calmly, gets more agitated (busier) towards the middle with smaller note values used, and ends calmly.

Improvising

In pairs improvise a piece using the four sets of notes from the In scale at the bottom of the page. The sets of notes should be performed in this order:

```
                4    4
            3             3
        2                       2
    1                               1
```

The piece should have a mountain shape and the same qualities and feeling as *Tamuke*. A similar effect may be created using the guidelines below.

Guidelines

1   Player 1 begins by improvising a short phrase using *only the four notes of set 1*:
   i   begin with the long note (indicated in heavy type). Approach it from the note in brackets underneath.
   ii   continue improvising your phrase using only the notes given
   iii end your improvised phrase with a long note, and nod to player 2 to begin.

2   Player 2 now builds on player 1's improvisation *using the notes of set 2* and keeping up the mood. Nod to player 1 when your phrase is complete.

3   Player 1 continues the improvisation *using the notes of set 3* and nods when their phrase is complete.

4   Both players continue to alternate improvisations in this way until the piece is finished.

Remember, the whole piece should get gradually higher and then lower. The music should become more agitated with smaller note values towards the top of the mountain.

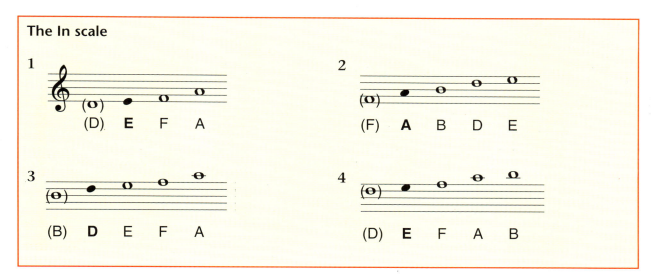

The In scale

1   (D) **E** F A

2   (F) **A** B D E

3   (B) **D** E F A

4   (D) **E** F A B

Listening to Etenraku: timbres into textures

Listen to *Etenraku* (tracks 38–39), an ancient ceremonial piece of Gagaku music played on ancient instruments, and follow the graphic score on the opposite page. This ensemble piece has many features and qualities similar to those of the other pieces listened to in this project.

However, the texture of *Etenraku* is much thicker. Despite this, each layer of *Etenraku* can still be heard clearly. This is because each layer has its own particular distinctive **timbre**, and only one of each instrument plays each layer. A description of each layer follows:

Layer	Instrument	Contribution to the music
melody	**ryūteki**: an early type of flute	performs a decorated version of the melody
	hichiriki: a double reed instrument with a very piercing sound	plays the melody
chord	**sho**: a type of mouth organ, sounds like a distant siren	plays high-pitched clusters of notes together as a chord
drone	**biwa**: a short-necked lute played with a plectrum	strums spread drone notes
counter-melody	**koto**: a zither-like instrument	plays a separated ostinato-like melody
percussion	**kakko**: a small double-headed drum that is suspended and hit with unpadded sticks	plays repeated notes evenly or accelerating
	shoko: a small suspended gong which has a metallic sound that is dampened	played at the beginning and end of each percussion pattern with the kakko
	taiko: a large double-headed drum that is suspended and hit with a padded stick	played in the middle and at the end of each percussion pattern

Japanese drummers

Etenraku graphic score

Sho

Ryūteki & hichiriki

Koto

Biwa

Shoko
Kakko
Taiko

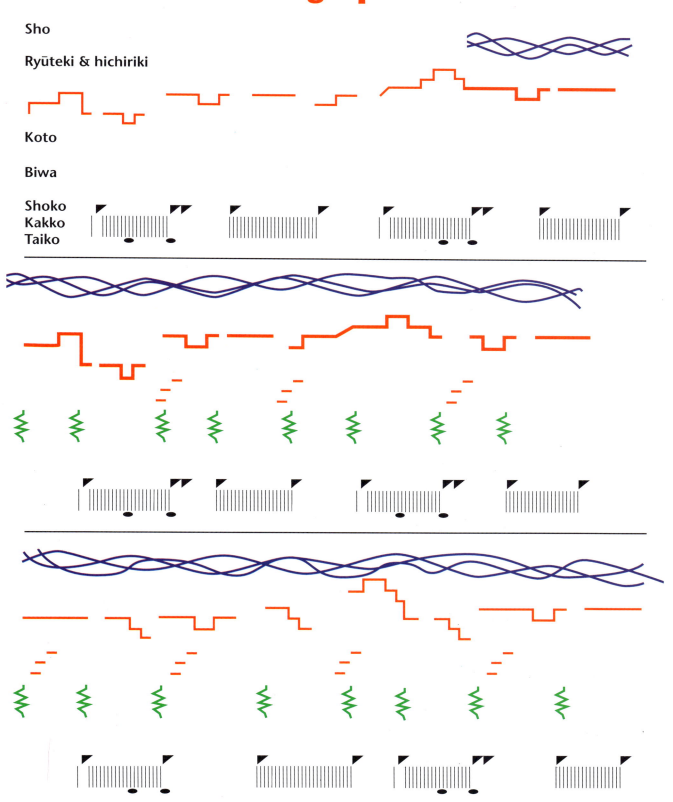

53

Kites

Pockriss

1   I will fly a yellow paper sun in your sky,
    When the wind is high, when the wind is high.
    I will float a silken silver moon near your window,
    If your night is dark, if your night is dark.

    Chorus
    In letters of gold on a snow-white kite,
        I will write 'I love you'
    And send it soaring high above you,
        For all to read.

2   I will scatter rice-paper stars in your heaven,
    If there are no stars, if there are no stars.
    All of these and seven wonders more will I fly,
    When the wind is high, when the wind is high.

Studying a baroque concerto

Lute concerto in D major by Antonio Vivaldi

A **concerto** is a piece of music composed for a solo instrument accompanied by an orchestra. It has always been a very popular **genre** (type of music) for performers, composers and audiences as the solo part is usually technically very difficult and allows the 'star' to show off their skill and musicianship. This lute concerto has three movements. The first and third movements are fast, contrasting with the slower second movement.

Antonio Vivaldi

Antonio Vivaldi (1678–1741) was an Italian who worked in Venice for a large part of his life. He excelled at composing concertos, and wrote nearly five hundred of them for lots of different solo instruments and also for small groups of solo instruments. He is probably best remembered for the famous set of four concertos for solo violin and string orchestra called *The four seasons*.

The solo concerto is a genre that developed during what is called the **baroque** period of musical history. The word 'baroque' describes music composed roughly from 1600–1750 with a number of special characteristics and stylistic features. You will learn more about these features later on in this project.

The solo instrument in this concerto is the **lute**. The lute was an important instrument for both solos and accompaniments during the sixteenth and seventeenth centuries, rather as the guitar is today. It is a plucked

Lute seen from the front

Lute seen from the side

stringed instrument with a very characteristic pear shape, similar to the guitar both in sound and in construction. By the end of the seventeenth century the lute had developed in size to require as many as 26–30 strings (see above).

Vivaldi's *Lute concerto in D* is accompanied by a small orchestra of strings and a harpsichord. The harpsichord is playing a part known as the **continuo**. The continuo player is expected to read from a skeleton score and work out the chords from a set of numbers called a figured bass. They then interpret those numbers to fill in and decorate the chords to thicken the texture of the music and support the overall structure.

The first movement of the *Lute concerto in D major* begins with a **ritornello** performed *tutti* which means it is played by everyone, the whole orchestra and the soloist. The word 'ritornello' means 'returning', and is used to describe a section of music that is often repeated throughout a concerto movement. The ritornello alternates with contrasting sections performed by the solo lute.

Project 6

Lute concerto in D – first movement

Vivaldi arr. CH

Work on this arrangement of the opening ritornello together as a class. It consists of three sections, labelled **A**, **B** and **C**. A fourth section – **D** – is also included on the score. It will be used later (see page 58). Perform sections A, B and C finishing at the word *Fine* (ending).

* This bracketed note belongs to Section C.

Improvisations in ritornello form

Improvisation is an important feature of baroque music. Composers often wrote only a 'skeleton' of their music and expected the performer to bring it to life by improvising around it. In this way no two performances of a piece were exactly the same.

Make your class performance of this ritornello more like Vivaldi's first movement by adding your own solo sections. Using the following guidelines, add several eight-bar solo improvisations to make your class performance longer.

1   Rehearse section D of the ritornello. Section D will be used to accompany the solo improvisations. Perform section D a number of times to familiarize yourself with it.
*Note: Section D is in D **major**. If a soloist chooses to improvise in D **minor** (see below), you must change section D so that all the F#s become Fs, and all the Bs become B♭s.*

2   Improvise an eight-bar solo using *either* the notes of the D major scale:

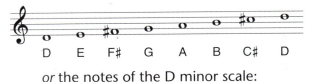

D   E   F#   G   A   B   C#   D

or the notes of the D minor scale:

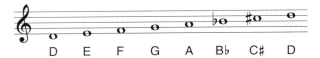

D   E   F   G   A   B♭   C#   D

- use rhythms similar to section A or B in your improvisation
- start and finish on the note D
- move mainly in steps
- if a note sounds wrong, move by step to another note.

Perform your class ritornello using the following structure. Add as many solo improvisations as you wish.

1 A	2 B	3 C	4 **D** solo improvisation accompanied by D
5 A	6 B	7 **D** solo improvisation accompanied by D	8 A

9 B	10 **D** solo improvisation accompanied by D	11 A	12 B	13 C

Some popular instruments of the baroque period

- harpsichord, organ
- lute, guitar
- viols → violin and cello
- oboe, bassoon, recorder → flute
- trumpets, horns, sackbuts
- timpani

An eighteenth-century harpsichord

Listening to the first movement

All but two parts of the first movement use one or more of the three sections **A**, **B** and **C** from the opening ritornello (see below):

Section A

Section B

Section C

Listen to the first movement of the *Lute concerto* (track 42) and answer the questions below:

1   The parts of the first movement are listed in the chart below. First copy out the chart. Next, beside each part fill in the sections heard from the opening ritornello (i.e. A, B, C, or new melody). The first one is done for you.

Parts		Sections
1	tutti	A, B, C
2	mainly lute and continuo	
3	tutti	
4	mainly lute and continuo	
5	tutti	
6	mainly lute and continuo	
7	tutti	
8	mainly lute and continuo	
9	tutti	
10	mainly lute and continuo	
11	tutti	

2   Below are three incomplete sentences: **a**, **b** and **c**, and three statements **i**, **ii**, and **iii**. Match each sentence with the correct statement.
Note: You may use a statement more than once.

sentences

a   The dynamics of the piece
b   The texture of the piece
c   The mood of the piece

statements

i   is/are virtually the same throughout.
ii   change(s) very gradually.
iii change(s) frequently.

3   The lute is a quiet instrument. In this movement how does Vivaldi make sure that it is heard above the other instruments of the orchestra?

4   Name another structure in which a melody alternates with contrasting material.

Lute concerto in D – second movement

Learning about dotted notes

Many of the quaver notes in the melody of the second movement have a dot placed after them. A dot tells us that each dotted note should be lengthened by half as much again.

This means that the note that follows each dotted quaver is made into a semiquaver so that the bar will add up to the time signature correctly. The semiquaver is shown by the double beam above the note. The resulting rhythm is quite jumpy.

Vivaldi arr. CH

Part 1

D F#G AD F#A F# E   A   A F#E DA F#E D

B A B B B A B B   C# C#B AC# C#B A

C# C#B AC# C#B A   A B A B A B A B   A G#F# E D C#B C# B C#

D F#G AD F#A F# E   B   B C#B A G F#E D

C# B A E F# F# E G F# GA DF# E D

Directing a performance from the harpsichord

Some musical features of the baroque period

a **contrast:**

   i   one to four solo instruments contrasted with the orchestra

   ii   slow movements alternated with fast movements in suites of dances

   iii   soft passages alternated with loud passages in the music.

b   orchestras were directed by the harpsichord player who also played the continuo part.

Part 2

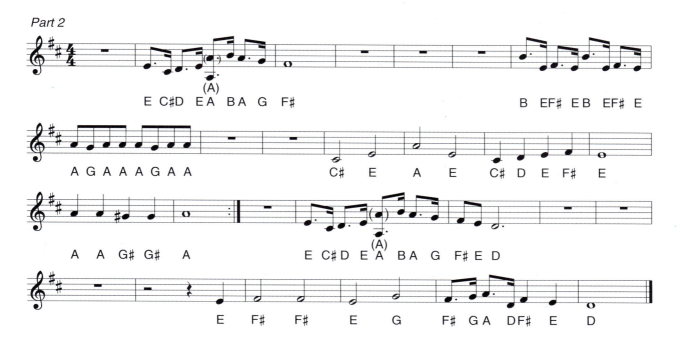

E C#D EA BA G F#   (A)   B EF# EB EF# E

A G A A A G A A   C# E A E C# D E F# E

A A G# G# A   E C#D EA BA G F#E D   (A)

E F# F# E G F# GA DF# E D

Part 3

F# AD F#A F#E D E A A

A DE DA DE D G#A B AG#F#E D C# E A E A B C# D

C# C# B C#   A A BAGF#EDC BAG

E F# F# E G F# GA DF# E D

Listening to the second movement

Like the first movement, the second movement from Vivaldi's *Lute concerto in D* also has a number of sections. Listen to the whole movement right through (track 43). This is performed by Julian Bream. Answer the following questions:

1   What are the features of the second movement that make it an effective contrast to the first movement? You could write about the tempo, dynamics, texture, and mood in your answer.

2   Describe what the string orchestra does in this movement. What does it add to the music?

3   What is the structure of this movement? Choose from the following:

i   AB   ii   ABA

iii AABA   iv   ABACADA

Five important styles of the baroque period

i   **concerto**: a work for a solo instrument and orchestra, or a group of two to four soloists and orchestra *(concerto grosso)*

Julian Bream playing the lute

ii   **opera**: a musical play with orchestra. It was composed as a series of solos known as arias and choruses, and the story of the play was told in a type of sung speech called *recitative*

iii   **oratorio**: an opera on a biblical story performed without actions or scenery

iv   **suite**: a group of contrasting dances played together as a set

v   **trio sonata**: a work for two violins with a *continuo* part played by cello and harpsichord or organ.

An Italian opera rehearsal about 1710

Listening to the third movement

The fast third movement of Vivaldi's *Lute concerto in D* has two beats in the bar. You can hear this clearly (track 44) because the beat is so definitely felt as 'left, right, *left*, right, *left*, right, *left*, right' etc. Before you answer the questions, listen to the music right through, and tap 'left, right, left, right, etc' with one finger silently on alternate knees until you are comfortably in time with the music. Now listen to the music again several times and answer the following questions:

1   The music has two beats in each bar. Is the time signature $\frac{2}{4}$ (simple time) or $\frac{6}{8}$ (compound time)?

2   The movement falls into several definite sections. Below is a partly completed grid showing the number of bars in each section. How many bars are there in each of the uncompleted sections?

section 1 15	section 2 19	section 3 ?	section 4 19
section 5 3	section 6 3	section 7 ?	section 8 19
section 9 3	section 10 ?	section 11 9	section 12 ?

3   Like the first movement, this third movement is in ritornello form. The ritornello form means that the contrasting sections are either played by the solo lute accompanied by the continuo or they are played by everybody (*tutti*). Sometimes the *tutti* starts or ends a section. Copy and complete the table below using the following descriptions to help you:

a   lute and continuo
b   tutti
c   tutti joins in towards the end
d   tutti begins and ends this section

Section	Description
1	**b** tutti
2	**a** lute and continuo; **c** tutti joins in towards the end
3	
4	
5	**b** tutti
6	**b** tutti
7	**c** tutti joins in towards the end
8	**d** tutti begins and ends this section
9	
10	
11	
12	

4   Many instrumental pieces composed in the baroque period ended with fast dance-like movements. Why does this movement make such a successful ending to the whole concerto?

Making comparisons

Listen to excerpts from two other concertos: *Clarinet concerto no 1* by Weber (track 45) and *Double concerto for saxophone, cello and orchestra* by Michael Nyman (track 46), and compare them with Vivaldi's *Lute concerto* and with each other.

Weber (1786–1826) wrote his clarinet concerto over a hundred years later than Vivaldi's *Lute concerto in D*, and Michael Nyman (b.1944) wrote his concerto in 1995. During this long period of time the concerto has changed and developed in a number of ways. What similarities and differences do you notice between the three works?

1   The concerto is primarily a piece of music to allow the soloist(s) to show off their technical skill and musicianship. How successful do you think each of these three compositions is in giving the soloist(s) a chance to 'show off'.
    Which of the three gives the most opportunity for showing off? Why do you think this is?

2   The role of the orchestra in the concerto has varied over the years from being an equal partner with the soloist to being just an accompanist. Write a short paragraph about the part the orchestra plays in each of these concertos.

3   Concertos are one of the most popular types of 'classical' music because audiences enjoy watching soloists as much as listening to them, and love to admire their amazing skill. Which of these three pieces do you think would sell the most records, and why?

Performing a cello concerto

Michael Nyman (right) at work